HIGH TREASON

IN

THE

I0151057

GARDEN

(The Conspiracy Against Your Flesh)

It's A Book

A Journal AND A Journey

The First "Idea", Was To Write This Book About The First Conspiracy Against Man In The Garden With Eve, Then Escalate It Against Treason That Was Carried Out Against Christ, Then Treason That Is Carried Out Against The Spirit And The Flesh Being The Traitor.

The Requirement Of Holiness Has Not Changed From The Old To The New Covenant; Only The Means Of Acquiring That Holiness Has Changed.

The Garden Is Where Every Thing Beautiful Was Created.

ACNOWLEDGEMENT

I Would Like To Thank My Lord And
Savior
Jesus Christ
For All That God Has Given Me
I Recognize That The Lord Gave Me
This Gift
Which Allows Me To Share With
Everyone That Participates In The
Reading Of The Literary Material That I
Produce Through The Commission Of
God
Thank You Lord God
I Will Forever Be Grateful
For Your Trust In Me

Pamela Denise Brown

Books Speak For You books may be ordered through
booksellers or by contacting:
Books Speak For You Educational Publishing
Booksspeakforyou.com
1-800-757-0598
The views expressed in this work are solely those of the
author.
Any illustration provided by iStock and such images are
being used for illustrative purposes.
Certain stock imagery © iStock.
ISBN: 978-1-64050-329-8

Library Of Congress PCN Number: 2017918402

Printed in the United States Of America

Introduction

"High Treason In The Garden, The Conspiracy Against Your Flesh".

God Wants You To Know, Just Like In The Garden, The Devil Is Still Conspiring And Trying To Kill And Destroy You. There Is A Conspiracy Against Your Flesh, With Your Flesh!!!

There Is A Conspiracy Against Your Create With Who You Were Created To Be, Because There Is Still A Conspiracy Against God.

God Said, In The Beginning Was The Word And The Word Was GOD And The Word Was With God...

AND

In Matthew, God's Word Was Made Flesh...

The Devil Is Coming Against The Word "Materialized" As Flesh, Which Is YOU And The Word Made Flesh, Which Is

"God In YOU".

This Read Is Powerful In Its Absolute Ability To Inform And Rescue You.

The Bible Says, We Perish For Lack Of Knowledge, Well,

"Here Comes The Light!!!".

Treason: The Crime Of Betraying One's Country, Especially By Attempting To Kill The Sovereign Or Overthrow The Government…

The Act Of Betraying Someone Or Something…

Conspiracy: A Secret Plan By A Group To Do Something Unlawful Or Harmful. The Action Of Plotting Or Conspiring.

Scriptural Read

Galatians 5:19-26King James Version

¹⁹ Now the works of the flesh are manifest, which are these; Adultery, fornication, uncleanness, lasciviousness,

²⁰ Idolatry, witchcraft, hatred, variance, emulations, wrath, strife, seditions, heresies,

²¹ Envyings, murders, drunkenness, revellings, and such like: of the which I tell you before, as I have also told you in time past, that they which do such things shall not inherit the kingdom of God.

²² But the fruit of the Spirit is love, joy, peace, longsuffering, gentleness, goodness, faith,

²³ Meekness, temperance: against such there is no law.

²⁴ And they that are Christ's have crucified the flesh with the affections and lusts.

²⁵ If we live in the Spirit, let us also walk in the Spirit.

²⁶ Let us not be desirous of vain glory, provoking one another, envying one another.

I'm Going To Run In The Spirit And Start This Book Again...

It's November 28, 2017 9:26 pm And God Is On The Throne, Jesus At His Right Hand...

I Will Write This Book In Ministering Format As I Am Typing And Talking To You...

Every Word That I Am Typing, I Want You To "Acknowledge" It, *As A Personal Conversation I Am Having With You*, In Hopes Of Getting You To Receive This Message, That It May Transform The Way You Think, What You Do And More Importantly What Will Now Be Priority In Your Life.

Let Me Run...

The First Act Of Treason Was Committed In The Garden...

The Garden Was The Place Where Everything Beautiful Was Made...

God Gave An Order And Spoke...

Satan However, Had Another Plan And That Plan Was To Overthrow The Word And Command Of The Sovereign God, Who Was The Government.

God Was The Only Existing Force Of Rulership, Dominion And Principality...

The Crime Of Betrayal Was Carried Out, Because The Conspiracy Against The Flesh, *Which Knew Not Who It Was*, Was None The Less Active In Its Pursuit To Be "Satisfied"...

Lord Help Me With This Please...

What I'm Trying To Say To You Is That The Flesh Acted As An Isolated Agent To Fill It's Appetite As Flesh, Because It Knew If Was Flesh In The Substance Reality...

Hallelujah And In That Reality, It Penetrated The Mind Of Satan, And The Conspiracy Between The Two Of Them Took Place...

The Conspiracy Against Your Flesh With Your Flesh.

You See The Bible Says:

In John 1, **1 In the beginning was the Word, and the Word was with God, and the Word was God.**

2 The same was in the beginning with God.

3 All things were made by him; and without him was not anything made that was made.

Come On In This Room…

Flesh Was Made…

The Conspiracy Against Your Flesh Enacted By The Act Of Treason To The Word Of God, Which Was "GOD"…

God Was The Word And Satan Came Against God In Word Form And Tempted Eve To Eat The Forbidden Fruit Of The Tree Of Knowledge…

Knowledge Of Flesh…

Knowledge Of Word…

Knowledge Of God As Word Being The Traitor To The Purpose Of The Creation Of Life…

It Was "High Treason In The Garden" The Place Where Everything Was Made Beautiful For The Glorifying Of God The Creator Of It All.

Then We Have Jesus…

The Conspiracy Against Who He Was And What He Was Sent To Do...

The Pre-Incarnate Christ...

Remember Christ Was Here In The Beginning And Has Always Been...

The Bible Says In John...

John 8:58 (KJV)

[58] Jesus said unto them, Verily, verily, I say unto you, Before Abraham was, I am.

Note: It Says... "Before Abraham Was, I AM...

Christ The I AM God...

Christ The I AM Sovereign...

Christ The I AM Ruler...

Christ The I AM King...

Christ The I AM Existing As I AM..
Self Existing In I AM...
AND God The Creator Of It All...

The I Am In I Am, Being I Am God, Christ, Absolute Existing…

Now I Know I'm All Over The Place And I Get It, Please Remember I Am Not Writing To Entertain You.. I Am Writing What God Is Pouring Into Me…

Jesus Was Nailed On A Cross…

High Treason Was Committed In The Garden Of Geysemane.

They Charged Jesus With Crimes He Did Not Do And In Doing So They Committed Treason Against God…

The Conspiracy As It Has Always Been From The Beginning Of Creation Was To Come Against Creation…

To Come Against What God Created…

To Come Against Good…

To Come Against Rulership…

To Come Against Authority…

To Come Against Sovereignty Of The Sovereign God…

High Treason In The Garden Was Committed And The Conspiracy Against Your Flesh Is Still Being Carried Out By Your Flesh, Against You In Your Flesh…

God However, Gave You All The Power To Fight…

To Battle, To Conquer And To Win!!!

They Nailed Jesus To A Cross AND He HUNG On A Tree On Calvary...

He Was Crucified And Because The Act Of Treason Was Committed Against The Flesh, The Flesh Had To Pay...

The Flesh Hung...

The Flesh Was Tortured...

The Flesh Was Beat...

The Flesh Was Whipped...

The Flesh Was Bruised...

The Flesh Was Nailed To The Cross AND Crucified...

The Conspiracy Against The Flesh Is Still Going On Today And Your Flesh Is Conspiring To Take You Down...

To Discourage You...

To Drive You Crazy...

To Make You Commit Suicide...

To Make You Kill Your Family...

To Make You Commit All Kinds Of Sin...

Why, Because The Conspiracy Is Against GOD!!!

The Creator Of Everything The Devil Hates And He Hates You...

The Bible Says In John 10: [10] The thief cometh not, but for to steal, and to kill, and to destroy: I am come that they might have life, and that they might have it more abundantly.

The "Key" Here Is To Understand Who The Thief Is... To Understand The Purpose Of The Thief And To Understand To Underlying Message...

Now I'm Still Running...

And Right Now I'm Going To Climb...

I Want To Talk A Little Bit About Flesh, But I Don't Want To Use The Merriam Dictionaries Version Of The Word Flesh As Defined: **1**.the soft substance consisting of muscle and fat that is found between the skin and bones of an animal or a human.
I Want To Go To The Metaphysical Meaning Of Flesh...

The Spiritual Meaning Of Its Purpose Of Existing And How In That Purpose, God Has A Purpose That He Still Wants Fulfilled.

God Wants The Flesh Mortified, Crucified And Understood As Spirit Not Covering...

The Flesh Acting As Flesh Desires...

The Flesh Acknowledging Flesh Surrenders And Learns...

It Exist...

It Understands...

It Submits...

It Denies...

It Learns And It's Consciousness Of It Is Understood In The Transformation Of The "Christ Like Mind"...

Flesh Is Understood In It's Right, Rightful Conception, Perception And Idea...

God Wants Us To Understand Who We Are...

Who We Belong To…

Where We Came From…

Why We Exist And What Will Be The Cause Of The End Of Our Existence If We Don't Surrender Ourselves To The Christ Like Mind And Understand The Process, The Journey And More Important The "Create"…

Most People Want To Talk And Minister About The Gospel AND I Get That…

Jesus Said To Preach The Gospel…
Jesus Told His Disciples To Go To The Ends Of The Earth And Preach The Gospel…
I Agree And I Concur…
However, That's Not The Mission Of This Book!!!

I Want You To Look At Your Life Differently From This Day Forward And If You're Like Me and Probably Every Other Human You've Asked Yourself On More Than One Occasion, Lord Why Am I Here…

Why Do I Exist...

Where Did I Come From...

What Is My Purpose On Earth...

What Will Happen To Me When I Die...

Why Do I Have To Die..

Why Is Life So Hard...

Is There Really A God...

AND On

AND On

AND On...

I Just Dropped By To Tell You In This Little Book, That There Is AND Has Always Been A Conspiracy Against Your Flesh And It DID NOT STOP Because Jesus Died For Your Sins...

It Did Not Stop, Because Jesus Rose…

It Did Not Stop, Because Jesus Was Crucified…
The Devil Is Still Trying To Kill You And He Is Using You Against You…

That Is Why You Must DIE In Your Present State And Be Born Again In The State Of Your "Understood" Create.

Why Do You Think God Said That He Created You In His Image…

Look… Surely You Don't Think The "Image" God Was And Is Talking About Has Anything To Do With Your Freckles, Your Hair Color, Your Long Legs, Your Brown Eyes Or Your Lips…

The "Image" God Is Talking About Is The Image Of The Spirit Create…
Existing Like Himself…

God Procreates Himself In Life So He Can Keep Seeing Himself AND Since He Is A Spirit…

For The Love Of God...

GOD WANTS TO SEE YOU IN SPIRIT...

The Spirit Of Him As Love...

The Spirit Of Him As Peace...

The Sprit Of Him As Joy...

The Spirit Of Him As Health...

And The Only Way God Can See You As Himself Is If You **BECOME** Who You Were Created To Be Before The Error...

Before Treason Was Committed...

Before The Conspiracy...

God Wants To See You In The Image Of The Thought That He Had When He Created You AND He Wants You To Utilize All The Tools And Armor He Gave To You In The Spirit When Jesus Died And Rose In Victory To Become That Image...

We Don't Need To Continue To Play Games With Ourselves...

As Long As You Live, The Adversary Will Try To Kill You...

As Long As You Live, The Adversary Will Try To Discourage You And Take You Down...

The *"Concentrate"* However, Should Not Be To Focus On What The Adversary Is Doing, But Who You Are In Creation...

You Need To Know Who You Are...

You Need To Know Who You Belong To...

And More Importantly You Need To Know That Not Only Was High Treason Committed In The Garden, It Was Also Committed During Your Birth...

The Conspiracy Against Your Flesh Is On Going And It Will Never End Until Your Demise..

Your Focus Should Continuously Be On Your Victory And As Such The Fruit That You Bare Needs To Reflect Christ...

Jesus Is A Wonder And God Through His Son Is Amazing...

God Set It Up That We Would Like Christ, Conquer, Endure And Win!!!

You Have To See It...

Just Look, Really Look At Yourself. Look At Your Life.

God Is A Bad God...

God Set It Up That We Would Prove To Be Gods, But The Only Way You Can Understand This And Live In The Win Is To First Be Born Again And Confess With Your Mouth That Jesus Christ Is Lord And Then To Have The Mind Of Christ.

I Beseech You To Pray And Ask God For A Christ Like Mind..

I Beseech You To Look At Life Through The Windows Of The Eyes Of The Creator.

Why Did God Say We Were Created In His Image?

Why Did God Say We Would Be Able To Tread On Serpents?

Why Did God Say We Would Drink Poison And It Wouldn't Harm Us?

Why Did God Said We Should Walk And Faint Not?

Why Did God Say We Would Do Greater Things?

AND Why Did God Say We Would Have Power?

I Think The Concentrate Should Be On Who We Are In The Creation Of God And Not Who We Are In The Vision Of Our Flesh Describe As:

1.the soft substance consisting of muscle and fat that is found between the skin and bones of an animal or a human.

This Is The LIE, This Is What Kills You, Destroys You, Distracts You, Lies To You, Misguides You, Leaves You Alone, Lonely, Sick, Poor And In Sin...

The Lie...

And

That Lie Committed And Is Still Committing Treason Against You To Overthrow The Governing Force In Your Life, *Which Is The Word Of God*, Which Is God.

The Conspiracy Is Active And Always Will Be...

Your Flesh In The Mind That Is Not "Christ Like" Has Unbeknown To You Teamed Up With Your Flesh And They Come Against Your Thoughts, Your Actions, Your Imagination...

They Influence You, They Lure You, They Seduce You, They Make You Feel Good And When They Have Had Their Way With You, They Leave You In Sin In Bad Standing With God, Confused, Lonely, Scarred, Regretful, Misinformed, Unhappy And Sometimes Suicidal.

Remember When God Said Everything He Created Was Good?

LOOK...

Genesis 1King James Version

1 In the beginning God created the heaven and the earth.

2 And the earth was without form, and void; and darkness was upon the face of the deep. And the Spirit of God moved upon the face of the waters.

3 And God said, Let there be light: and there was light.

4 And God saw the light, that it was good: and God divided the light from the darkness.

5 And God called the light Day, and the darkness he called Night. And the evening and the morning were the first day.

[6] And God said, Let there be a firmament in the midst of the waters, and let it divide the waters from the waters.

[7] And God made the firmament, and divided the waters which were under the firmament from the waters which were above the firmament: and it was so.

[8] And God called the firmament Heaven. And the evening and the morning were the second day.

[9] And God said, Let the waters under the heaven be gathered together unto one place, and let the dry land appear: and it was so.

[10] And God called the dry land Earth; and the gathering together of the waters called he Seas: and God saw that it was good.

[11] And God said, Let the earth bring forth grass, the herb yielding seed, and the fruit tree yielding fruit after his kind, whose seed is in itself, upon the earth: and it was so.

[12] And the earth brought forth grass, and herb yielding seed after his kind, and the tree yielding fruit, whose seed was in itself, after his kind: and God saw that it was good.

[13] And the evening and the morning were the third day.

[14] And God said, Let there be lights in the firmament of the heaven to divide the day from the night; and let them be for signs, and for seasons, and for days, and years:

[15] And let them be for lights in the firmament of the heaven to give light upon the earth: and it was so.

[16] And God made two great lights; the greater light to rule the day, and the lesser light to rule the night: he made the stars also.

[17] And God set them in the firmament of the heaven to give light upon the earth,

[18] And to rule over the day and over the night, and to divide the light from the darkness: and God saw that it was good.

[19] And the evening and the morning were the fourth day.

[20] And God said, Let the waters bring forth abundantly the moving creature that hath life, and fowl that may fly above the earth in the open firmament of heaven.

[21] And God created great whales, and every living creature that moveth, which the waters brought forth

abundantly, after their kind, and every winged fowl after his kind: and God saw that it was good.

²² And God blessed them, saying, Be fruitful, and multiply, and fill the waters in the seas, and let fowl multiply in the earth.

²³ And the evening and the morning were the fifth day.

²⁴ And God said, Let the earth bring forth the living creature after his kind, cattle, and creeping thing, and beast of the earth after his kind: and it was so.

²⁵ And God made the beast of the earth after his kind, and cattle after their kind, and every thing that creepeth upon the earth after his kind: and God saw that it was good.

²⁶ And God said, Let us make man in our image, after our likeness: and let them have dominion over the fish of the sea, and over the fowl of the air, and over the cattle, and over all the earth, and over every creeping thing that creepeth upon the earth.

²⁷ So God created man in his own image, in the image of God created he him; male and female created he them.

²⁸ And God blessed them, and God said unto them, Be fruitful, and multiply, and replenish the earth, and subdue it: and have dominion over the fish of the sea,

and over the fowl of the air, and over every living thing that moveth upon the earth.

[29] And God said, Behold, I have given you every herb bearing seed, which is upon the face of all the earth, and every tree, in the which is the fruit of a tree yielding seed; to you it shall be for meat.

[30] And to every beast of the earth, and to every fowl of the air, and to every thing that creepeth upon the earth, wherein there is life, I have given every green herb for meat: and it was so.

[31] And God saw every thing that he had made, and, behold, it was very good. And the evening and the morning were the sixth day.

And IT Was Good...

Light Was Good!!!

Day Was Good!!!

Night Was Good!!!

The Animals Were Good!!!

AND

Man Was Good!!!

It Was Good...

Then High Treason In The Garden And The Act Of Betrayal To Overthrow The Sovereign God And His Governing Word Manifested And Sought Out To Conspire Against Man, Against Man's Flesh ...

The Conspiracy Like I Said Was The Flesh Word, Because It Knew No Other Existence Than To Know It As Word Not Actual Substance, But Word...

And That Word, Triggered The Curiously, Which Worked With The Flesh Against The Flesh Unknown And Lured It, Seduced It, Put Imagination And Wondering In The Mind Of It And Finally Had Its Way With It In The Conspiracy And Revealed Itself To It At What It Was...

But NOT In The Spiritual Defined Meaning In The Flesh Of The Flesh That Was Never Suppose To Know Itself In That Sense And Now Today The Battle Is Perpetual, Because The Conspiracy Is Ramped And Understood.

Sometimes If We Really Understand The Underlying Purpose Of A Thing And It's Origin We Can See It

From A Different Perspective And Fight It With That Perspective.

If We Stop And Really Think About Our Salvation And What That Means, Our Existence And What That Means...
Our Purpose And What That Means...
Then, We Can SEE With The Eyes Of Our Spiritual Existence And Conquer The Error That Was Laid On After The Creation Of The GOOD THING God Created When He Created Us...

God Has The Master Plan And Although He Destroyed Sodom And Gomorah And Told Noah To Build The Ark, Which Consequently Resulted In Just His Family Surviving, His Agenda, Purpose And Plan For The Outcome Of His Creation Is Still The Same.

God Put Us Together And Gave Us Will...

God Gave Us Choice And I Can Only Imagine The Creator Of Such A Creation, Looking And Wondering When Are They Going To Figure It Out...

When Are They Going To Figure Out...

"Who They Are"...

"What They Are..."

AND

 "Why They're Here"...

God Is Probably Saying, I Have Given Them Everything AND Although Treason In The Garden Was Committed Against My Word...

AND

Against My Creation, I Gave My Son As A Ransom For Their Lives...

My Son Died For Them...

My Son Rose For Them...

AND

My Son Was An LIVING Example Of Who I Created Them To Be...

An Example Is A Pattern, A Model, An Ideal, A Paradigm, And A Standard...

Jesus Was A Living Example...

We Must Stop Seeing Jesus Just As Savior...

Jesus Was More Than That...

Jesus Was God's Word That Came Alive...

Jesus Was God Victorious Against The Act Of Treason...

Jesus Was God Conquer Against The Conspiracy, Because He Conquered Sin...

LOOK...
2 Corinthians 5:21King James Version (KJV)
[21] For he hath made him to be sin for us, who knew no sin; that we might be made the righteousness of God in him.

Are You Kidding Me...

Do You NOT Understand...
Although The Conspiracy Still Exist To Kill, Destroy AND Steal, Just As Jesus Was Victorious, We Are Too...

It Doesn't Stop Because You Acknowledge It...
The Acknowledgment Of If Should Enact Power...
The Acknowledgement Of It Should Enact Praise...
The Acknowledgment Of It Should Enact Trust...

It Should Enact Surety...

You Need To Be Sure Of Who You Are And When You Waiver From Your Create, Your DNA, Your Genealogy, You Put Your Life At Risk To Be Ceased By The Act Of Treason And The Conspiracy Against Your Flesh Wins...

Do Not Be Fooled, Life Is Bigger Than You...

But Not Bigger Than God...

There Is No Escape In Life, But Through Death Of The Flesh And Then The Crossover Occurs And In That Life, Whether In Hell Or Heaven Your Created Image Is Disclosed Visually To You...

The Purpose However, For This Book Is That Your Create Be Exposed To You In Mind...

In Christ...

In Image Of The Born Again Experience With "That Understanding'...

BORN AGAIN...

Although, We Were Born In Sin And Life Laid The Layers On, Because We Perhaps Sought Not The "Truth", We Did Not Understand Our Need To Repent…

Salvation Was Offered Through The Acceptance Of Christ And In Accepting Christ Through The Covenant Agreement, We Were Saved…
NEW FLASH… It Does Not Stop There…

I Beckon You Please For The Love Of God **STOP** Acting Like Just Because You Accept Christ All Your Troubles Will End…

That's The Beginning…
The Beginning Of The New Life That Must Be Proved Victorious To You Through Your Journey In It..

Through You Process Of It…
Your Understanding AND Your Transformation…
It's God Being God And If You're The "Creator" Of Anything, You Know You Get Joy Out Of Watching What You Created Perform To Do Just What You Created It To Do….

Imagine Ford, After The Creation Of The Car And It Drove...

Imagine The Feeling He Had.

God Wants To Be Glorified In Our Lives And The Only Way He Can Be Glorified Is, If We Live The Way We Were Created To Live And Live In His Will.

We Have To Start Being Smart About This...

I Believe And I'll Say It Again, I "Believe" Jesus Is Soon To Come And My Prayer Now Is Lord, Please Let Me Be Ready...

I'm Treating Everyday Like A Task, Strategically Moving Through It...

Now That I Understand "High Treason Was Committed In The Garden" AND There Is A "Conspiracy Against My Flesh", I Act Like I Understand It...

What Is The Purpose Of Knowing Something And Acting And Living Like You Don't Know?

You're Only Playing Tricks On Yourself…

Remember The Kids Use To Say,
"You Better Act Like You Know"
OR
How About This…
"Fake It To You Make It"…

Maybe In Your Faking It, You'll Actually Get It And "Grab A Hold Of Yourself" (another one of my books)…

Please Get It Together…

When You Do, God Will Know And Let Me Just Say This, Please Don't Expect No Special "Acknowledgement" For Something You Should Already Be Doing..

Of Course God Is A Rewarder Of Them That Diligently Seek Him, So Don't Ware Yourself Out Praying For The Inevitable…

The Bible Says Seek Ye FIRST The Kingdom Of God, Which For Me Is Righteousness And Everything Else Will Be Added…

LOOK…

Matthew 6:33King James Version (KJV)

[33] But seek ye first the kingdom of God, and his righteousness; and all these things shall be added unto you.

All You Have To Do Is Get On Board With God And Everything You Need And Desire Will Be Added…

There Are More Important Things In Life Than Cars, Houses And All The Other Material Things We Pursue.

I Get It… I Want All Those Things Too, But Most Importantly I Want To Win With God…

I Want To Be Holy…

The Word Says Be Ye Holy For I Am Holy…

I'm Constantly Trying To Correct Myself With My Conscious Mind In Christ...

The Bible Says Thy Word Have I Hid In My Heart...

LOOK...

Psalm 119:11King James Version (KJV)

[11] Thy word have I hid in mine heart, that I might not sin against thee.

The Catch Here Is...
You Can't Hide The Word, If You Don't Know The Word.

I Invite You This Day To Learn The Word Of God And Hide The Truth In Your Heart That You Might Not Sin Against God...

Remember, When You Sin, You Don't Sin Against Anybody But God, So DON'T Let Anyone Convince You That You Have.

Remember David's Prayer After He Sinned Against Besheba...

He Said... ***Against You Lord Have I Sinned And Done This Evil In Thy Sight...***

LOOK...

AND After You Look, Lets Pray This Prayer And Start Over Again With The Knowledge That There Is A On-Going "Conspiracy" Against Your Flesh...

It Doesn't Even Matter...

You Got The Victory...

We Are Going To Look At Our "Create" From A Whole Different Perspective...

High Treason Is Constantly Being Committed Against God's Word And His Creation...

He Is The Absolute God And Because Satan Wanted To Be Him, He Launched An Attack On His Word, But Jesus Showed Us How To "Back It Up" Indeed Through The Crucifying Of His FLESH...

AND

Likewise, Our Flesh Must Also Be Crucified.

Glory To God, We Have The Victory...

Now, You Can Stop Crying...

Stop Complaining...

AND

Learn Who You Are....

Learn What You Are...

AND

Learn Purpose.

Be Ye Lifted Up Always In The Spirit Of Truth.

I Hope You Enjoyed This Writing.

I Enjoyed Writing It...

I Added Scriptures On How To Conquer And Overcome Sin In The Next Section.

It's Now 11:41 pm

November 28, 2017...

Scriptures

On

How To Conquer

AND

Overcome Sin

1 Corinthians 10:13King James Version (KJV)

[13] There hath no temptation taken you but such as is common to man: but God is faithful, who will not suffer you to be tempted above that ye are able; but will with the temptation also make a way to escape, that ye may be able to bear it.

1 John 2King James Version (KJV)

2 My little children, these things write I unto you, that ye sin not. And if any man sin, we have an advocate with the Father, Jesus Christ the righteous:

² And he is the propitiation for our sins: and not for ours only, but also for the sins of the whole world.

³ And hereby we do know that we know him, if we keep his commandments.

⁴ He that saith, I know him, and keepeth not his commandments, is a liar, and the truth is not in him.

⁵ But whoso keepeth his word, in him verily is the love of God perfected: hereby know we that we are in him.

⁶ He that saith he abideth in him ought himself also so to walk, even as he walked.

⁷ Brethren, I write no new commandment unto you, but an old commandment which ye had from the beginning. The old commandment is the word which ye have heard from the beginning.

⁸ Again, a new commandment I write unto you, which thing is true in him and in you: because the darkness is past, and the true light now shineth.

⁹ He that saith he is in the light, and hateth his brother, is in darkness even until now.

¹⁰ He that loveth his brother abideth in the light, and there is none occasion of stumbling in him.

¹¹ But he that hateth his brother is in darkness, and walketh in darkness, and knoweth not whither he goeth, because that darkness hath blinded his eyes.

¹² I write unto you, little children, because your sins are forgiven you for his name's sake.

¹³ I write unto you, fathers, because ye have known him that is from the beginning. I write unto you, young men, because ye have overcome the wicked one. I write unto you, little children, because ye have known the Father.

¹⁴ I have written unto you, fathers, because ye have known him that is from the beginning. I have written unto you, young men, because ye are strong, and the word of God abideth in you, and ye have overcome the wicked one.

¹⁵ Love not the world, neither the things that are in the world. If any man love the world, the love of the Father is not in him.

¹⁶ For all that is in the world, the lust of the flesh, and the lust of the eyes, and the pride of life, is not of the Father, but is of the world.

¹⁷ And the world passeth away, and the lust thereof: but he that doeth the will of God abideth for ever.

¹⁸ Little children, it is the last time: and as ye have heard that antichrist shall come, even now are there many antichrists; whereby we know that it is the last time.

19 They went out from us, but they were not of us; for if they had been of us, they would no doubt have continued with us: but they went out, that they might be made manifest that they were not all of us.

20 But ye have an unction from the Holy One, and ye know all things.

21 I have not written unto you because ye know not the truth, but because ye know it, and that no lie is of the truth.

22 Who is a liar but he that denieth that Jesus is the Christ? He is antichrist, that denieth the Father and the Son.

23 Whosoever denieth the Son, the same hath not the Father: he that acknowledgeth the Son hath the Father also.

24 Let that therefore abide in you, which ye have heard from the beginning. If that which ye have heard from the beginning shall remain in you, ye also shall continue in the Son, and in the Father.

25 And this is the promise that he hath promised us, even eternal life.

26 These things have I written unto you concerning them that seduce you.

²⁷ But the anointing which ye have received of him abideth in you, and ye need not that any man teach you: but as the same anointing teacheth you of all things, and is truth, and is no lie, and even as it hath taught you, ye shall abide in him.

²⁸ And now, little children, abide in him; that, when he shall appear, we may have confidence, and not be ashamed before him at his coming.

²⁹ If ye know that he is righteous, ye know that every one that doeth righteousness is born of him.

45 Day Journal

Use This Half Of The Book And Journal 45 Days Walking In

The Light Of The Knowledge

Of The Conspiracy Against Your Flesh

Write Down Your Discoveries

AND

After The 45 Days Of Journaling

Keep Going And Write Again

THIS TIME

Journal Your Journey

When You Read Your Progression

You'll Understand Your Battle

_____

_____

_____

_____

_____

_____

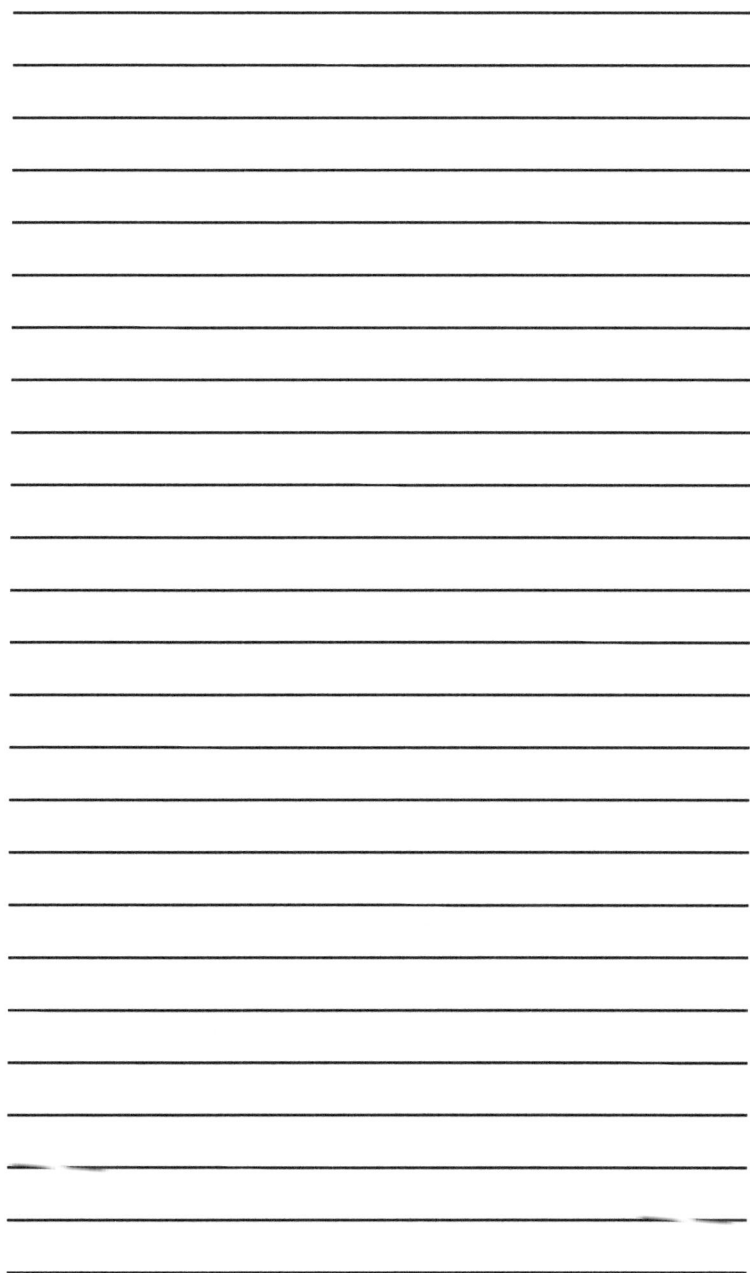

Journal Your Journey

And

Let The

Journey

Begin

-

_____

_____

_____

_____

_____

_____

_____

_____

_____

_____

_____

_____

_____

_____

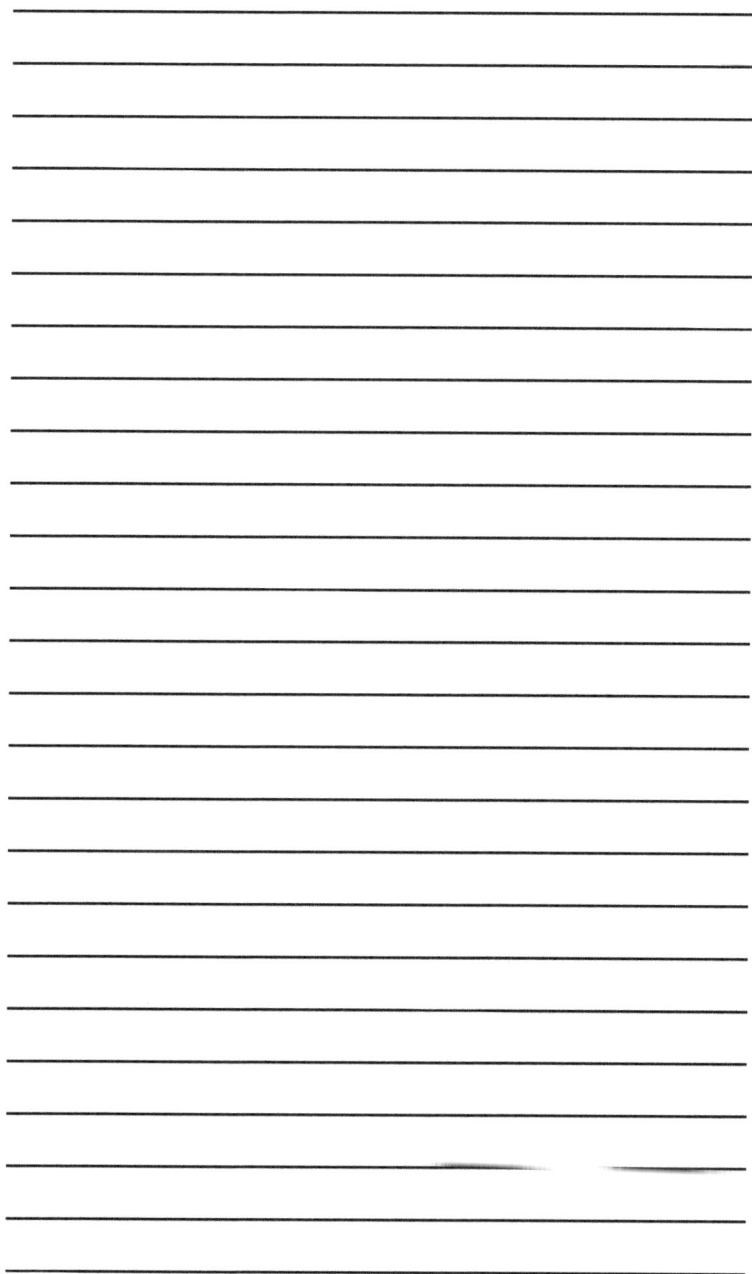

Thank You
For Purchasing
This Book
I Hope It Helped You

Pamela Denise Brown

I Released This Book

Christmas Day,

Monday, December 25, 2017

Happy Birthday Jesus

I Dedicate This Book To You

Published By Books Speak For You Publishing

Specializing In 3, 7 & 21 Day Publishing
Publishing In Over 100 Languages

Printed In The United States

www.Booksspeakforyou.com

1-800-757-0598

1-800-757-0598

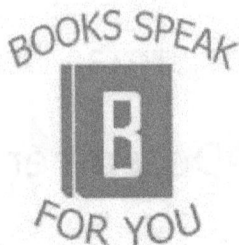

Pamela Denise Brown, Author

Creator Of Smart Books And Christian Books For Kids

267-318-8933

www.ingramcontent.com/pod-product-compliance
Lightning Source LLC
LaVergne TN
LVHW051126080426
835510LV00018B/2251